The

ULTIMATE

BUSINESS CARD

Grow Your
Business and Income
Faster, Better & Easier

By Matthew D. Miglin, PhD

Table of Contents

~ The Instant Business Revolution

Like the Wild West, gone are the days when you needed to hire expensive professionals to do all your business cards, brochures, stationery, letterhead, graphics, pictures, media, press releases, contracts, websites, bookkeeping, postcard mailings, flyers, videos, CDs, DVDs, and even your books.

It seems only a few years ago a business man or woman would be left with hundreds of business cards, brochures, letterhead, etc., from expensive print jobs that were of no value. What appeared at the time to be cheap, based on printing larger quantities, now appears to have actually cost a lot more than originally estimated because of the number of copies which were never used.

Welcome to the new Instant Business revolution! Modern technology has brought with it the advent of desktop publishing, inexpensive color laser printers, desktop computers, inexpensive software, templates, unlimited how-to resources online, quality inexpensive camera equipment, online recording, CD/DVD burners, as well as POD (print on demand: print houses capable of printing just one book at a time, or as many as needed). These new products and services make it accessible to the masses to have a big-business image on a small-business budget.

Instant business with the potential of instant income has changed the world of business overnight. What used to take weeks and months now happens almost instantly. Never before in history could a person decide today to start a business and in 24 to 48 hours have all the trappings of a veteran company: customized professional-looking business cards, brochures, web sites, and company voice mail.

This revolution is creating instant income for many without the need for renting a big office with staff and lots of startup capital. This is the age of the Instant Business and it is here to stay. What an exciting time to be in business.

This all appears to be good, and it is, but there is a problem. Many business owners are still conducting business the same way they have for years at a lower level of excellence and professionalism than they could have. They are rushing to market so fast they are missing key ingredients to effective marketing. Some business owners are still using obsolete sales tools, such as the tired old business card— a business tool that has hardly changed in decades.

Wait a minute—don't we want our business to stand out and look different from the competition? *Yes!* However, if you miss certain key ingredients, not even the best-looking brochure, business card, or web site will give your potential clients enough reason to give you a second look, much less do business with you.

Business requires differentiation and a little aggressiveness to expand and survive today. What follows are the keys to *The Ultimate Business Card,* starting with *you*. Since you are your prospect's first impression of your business, **YOU** are the first thing that needs work!

After you and your business image are clear, work begins on the other side of your business—the one that's rarely utilized and often neglected—and help you transform a mediocre business into an outstanding and profitable empire.

This book will give you the tools that can get you noticed and give you the credibility you need, like adding a book to your marketing equation. Come along and together we'll follow the best of the best, helping you add, "I'm the author of…" to your presentation.

~ You Are an Asset

Did you know that most businesses put more into their business card than they do into themselves? They forget that the best spokesperson for their company is themselves. I guarantee you will sell more with *you* than with your business card. Matter of fact, in my last business I went the last four years without a business card and *still* did over a million dollars in sales each year. That's because I understand that *I* am my best business card. If they don't buy *me*, they will never look at my sales materials.

Because you are your best business card, the purpose of this book is to <u>expand and brand you,</u> and your business, with your target market. You see...*who you are* speaks *volumes* to your prospects. Who you are speaks louder than any piece of paper with your name on it. Prospects buy *you* before they ever buy your business, product, or service.

No one is as passionate and enthusiastic about your business as you are. Your energy and spirit reach out far beyond your body and draw people to you—people who want to do business with you.

It's the principal of the Law of Attraction—you attract to you who you are and what you desire. People will rarely purchase based only on a great product or service. They buy primarily after building a relationship of trust. They buy the *person* before they ever buy the business, product, or service being offered.

Knowing that, you need to look at yourself and determine what kind of impression you are making. If you are your business card, how are people remembering you and what you do? Are you leaving them with a profound impression of you? If not, then you need to reevaluate your personal presentation and how you come across to others. You matter, so take care of you.

When you recognize that you are your business card first, then it will matter little what media or marketing material you provide to people to stay in contact with you. When it's you they buy, they will want to stay in touch, and will forgive any mistakes or problems much more easily. Relationships will make you money. Don't miss out on making your clients into your friends. Because friends tell other friends about people they like doing business with *first*, and about companies, products or services *second*. Make yourself a household name. Make YOU *The Ultimate Business Card*.

"Unaided recall and top-of-the-mind awareness are excellent ways to measure name recognition."

Dave Young, Branding Blog

~ Name and Face Recognition

Do your prospects know your face? Do they remember your name? If they don't, it is time to change that. If you were like me, you were told it is egotistical to put your name on everything and put your face on your books, brochures, websites, postcards, etc. It is just not what people 'do.' That's what I was told, but now I understand that I missed out on a valuable advertising space on my book covers, brochures, and websites. A missed opportunity also means missed revenue.

I am here to tell you that you want to do everything you can to have prospects remember your name and face so much that they see you everywhere they go and are unable to forget about you. In order for customers to not forget about you, they need to see or hear your name at least once every three months. Putting your face on your book cover is great because every time they move it or pick up your book they will think of you.

Your marketing objective for the next year should be to saturate your target market with your name and face so they think of you today, tomorrow, and as often as possible until they need your product or services again.

"There is only ONE YOU, so make your one-of-a-kind light shine for the whole world to see."

Matthew D. Miglin, PhD

~ Brand Yourself

As they grow, most companies will want to create a brand image. I say if you want to grow better, faster, and easier, create a spokesperson for your company, preferably you, and then *brand yourself as the company icon*. Make your face and name stand out and get it in front of the masses.

People remember people more easily than they do company names, products, or services. You want them to want to get to know you and have a lifetime relationship with you. They want to know that, if needed, you will be there to help them and meet their needs. Companies, products, and services are cold and non-relational. People prefer to deal with people.

If you catch hold of this truth you will watch your brand double overnight. In all instances (other than a few exceptions and mega organizations with unlimited marketing budgets) this works almost every time. Just look at video—if you add it to your website, you almost double your sales conversions. It's simply because people want to deal with a live person, not with an impersonal entity; they want to deal with *you*. Brand you, and watch your business grow.

"I will follow an enthusiastic and passionate person almost anywhere."

Matthew D. Miglin, PhD

~ What's in a Name?

The name you use is everything. You want it to be hard to forget. Next to a great company name, you need an outstanding domain name and probably more than one. I personally have dozens of domain names that I use, and you should, too. They are a cheap way (less than $10 per year) to secure valuable 'real estate' in the right name.

In addition to reserving domain names for your book and company, reserve your own personal name as well.

I also recommend using only dot **com** or dot **net** as they still tend to get higher search engine rankings, plus that is what most people are accustomed to seeing. When you are in search of the right domain name, just add more words until you find those available to purchase. (i.e., if you want, for example, coffeetables.com and it is unavailable, try searching for a name by adding additional words to it, such as coffeetablesforme.com or mybestcoffeetables.com). The choices are endless, but be creative and get the best domain name that will be hard for prospects to forget. Get yours today.

To get cheap domain names, visit: www.MattMiglin.com/resources

~ Website Value

It is commonplace today to have a website. If you don't have one, you better get one—*today!* You can set up a simple website yourself for as little as $10 a month and have your business accessible 24/7 so you can make money while you sleep.

There are no more excuses to not have your own website and to allow it to expand your marketing reach to the world. One thing you need to add to your website is a video. It doesn't even need to be fancy–just clear and understandable. Video conversions are doubling website sales and list building, so take advantage of it now. Enough said. Just get your website and video up to build your business faster.

For cheap websites go to:

www.MattMiglin.com/resources

"Are you still using an obsolete business card as your primary prospecting tool?"

Matthew D. Miglin, PhD

~ Obsolete Marketing

The age of the traditional paper business card is over, done, finished; it's obsolete. It doesn't work effectively any more. Just like the hammer for the contractor, its days are numbered. Most contractors now are using a nail gun to drive nails, not a hammer.

Out of all the business cards you hand out without saying anything, how many actually come back as sales? Few, if any, in most cases. Why? Everyone else is using a business card, too. So how are you different and how are you to make a lasting impression and be long remembered?

If you're like me, you have stacks of business cards rubberbanded together all over your office that never get looked at again. There are lots of businesses with great products and services that get lost with everyone else's business cards.

If you don't mind getting lost in the crowd, continue using the paper business card that has not changed in decades. It is time for a change and time to use a much more powerful marketing tool, like a book. Anyone who knows anything about marketing should write a book.

As for me and my office, we will use our book as our *Ultimate Business Card*.

"Would you like to experience the power of unlimited influence? Then write a book."

Matthew D. Miglin, PhD

~ Power of a Book

The next best thing to *you* is a book you have written. Your book is a reflection of you and your company. It is the perfect package for prospects to take you home with them. Just like the Bible is a reflection of who God is, our book lets people know us and have a constant reminder of us in their office or home.

A book gives a prospect additional time to get to know more about you and your company. A book is a continuation of your brief meeting or network experience with your prospect. It is also a continuation of your conversation long after you have met. It builds confidence and trust in you. The book becomes an extension of you; building this relationship even when you are not present. *Now that's power!* No business card does that. A book has power to continue the dialogue with your prospect even when you're not there, and proves that you are the best person for the job or with whom to do business.

Your book is better than a website because it is tangible and does not need to be opened up online. A book is always present with your cover begging them to read more about you. A book will change your life and your business. Get your book done *soon*. You will never want to prospect or network again without it.

When you need help with your book, visit: www.ExpertSelfPublishing.com

"Credibility is the foundation for everything. You can be liked, but lack credibility, and you'll lose sales. You can be assertive, but lack credibility, and you'll torpedo yourself. You can even know your buyer on a personal level, but lack credibility in your business and they'll always find ways to avoid doing business with you."

Brandon Hull
Sales Professional Coach

~ Instant Credibility

When you are properly branding yourself and using a book as your business card, you gain instant credibility. Why? Because as a book author you are perceived to be an expert on the subject at hand. A book gives you natural credibility and expert status. That's why, on the news, most guests are authors on the subject. Could that be *you* as the regional expert in your industry?

Books can change lives, incomes, and businesses overnight. You must become an author if you want to grow your business and income faster and bigger. Look at many of the wealthiest business owners you have heard of—they all have authored books: Donald Trump, Loral Langermeir, Robert Kiyosaki, Warren Buffet, Robert Allen, Zig Ziglar, Brian Tracy, Dale Carnegie, John Gray, John Maxwell, etc. The list goes on and on. You will see that the best of the best are authors of books.

Now it's *your* turn to become an author. *You can do it.* Just begin with a single step closer (i.e., make an outline of possible chapters, write the last page of the book, or just start with the title and subtitle). Begin with the end in mind, but at all costs, *just begin*.

"Your book can generate more income and opportunities than any college degree on earth."

Matthew D. Miglin, PhD

~ Better than a Degree

In our society today, we have placed a high value on the necessity to have a degree, and if possible a masters or doctorate degree. We say we value it because someone with a degree usually gets hired before someone without one. Even if you are smarter than someone with a degree, in most cases, the person with the degree wins. We also see this reflected in the compensation they are given. The higher the degree, the more they will, as a rule, be paid: 10%, 20%, 30%, even 100% or more.

A degree doesn't mean you are smarter than anyone else and does not express that you are an expert in any way, yet we hold this piece of paper in high esteem.

If this is the case with a single piece of paper from an educational institution, then what is the value of being the author of a book with *lots* of pieces of paper? Enormous! Massive! Major!

With a book, you are not only perceived as the expert and treated like one, you also get *instant credibility* and celebrity status. A PhD rarely gets free publicity, but authors get it every day of the week. Authors are paid differently than those with degrees. An author can see 100%, 500%, 1000% and often over 2,000% more in compensation than someone of equal age with a degree.

Take it one step further: an author can command outrageous compensation and not even have a high school diploma. How's *that* for power?

Yes, a book is better and more profitable than a degree. A book is less expensive than a college education and can be accomplished in four *months* rather than four to eight *years*. That is valuable time and money lost that could have been spent on building wealth and creating multiple books to help an unlimited number of people with your message.

~ Never Tossed or Lost

Your book is a long-term tool to be passed around, not thrown away. Unless a book is terrible, no one throws books away. We share them, reference them, write in them, and we generally keep them for a lifetime or close to it. A traditional business card, on the other hand, can get misplaced, left in an endless pile, or tossed in the trash within hours.

Even if a book gets put on a book shelf, the spine stands as a constant reminder that its content—your wisdom—is always within reach. Sometimes books are left in the bathroom, on the coffee table, in the car or a desk, but rarely ever get lost, tossed, or forgotten. When you give someone a book, it has a certain perceived value of $10, $15, $20 or more, while a business card is worth only a nickel or so. If you were a prospect, which would you hang on to longer: a book or a business card? If you are like me, I throw out quite a few business cards or I put them in an endless stack of other cards, never to be looked at again. The question is, what message are you sending to your prospect when you meet for the first time? Are you investing 5 cents or $20 into this new relationship? If you are competing with someone like me who has a book, I win almost every time.

What will *your* next business card be? I think you get the point.

"If you want an extraordinary life and income, you need to get published."

Matthew D. Miglin, PhD

~ Publish or Perish

In this information-rich moment in time, we are bombarded daily with direct and indirect marketing pieces. Whether it is our flooded email inbox, our snail mailbox, the online Internet ads, radio or TV ads, we have to agree, it is more than we want and more than we can afford to spend time on. We have become tone deaf to this glut of information.

As a result, our effectiveness in marketing today is reduced and our sales suffer as more companies saturate the market with more and more information for consumers to wade through—and the consumers become more confused and less decisive. So how can you stand out? How do you get noticed in this information-rich age? The answer: get published and do it *now*.

If you want to be noticed and stand out in the crowd, getting your name in print puts you in the top 5% of businesses and individuals who thrive today. Not only should you get your book out, but you should submit articles online to article submission sites that will get them exposed to multiple sites on the Internet. An article could be as little as two or three paragraphs of information about a topic related to your business or industry. Articles work well, blogs even better, and books best. Don't get lost in the chaos; publish today and leave your competition in the dust.

"Give yourself a pay raise.......write a book!"

Matthew D. Miglin, PhD

~ Double Your Income

Are you ready for a pay raise? Are you searching for something to increase your sales and increase your income? Then look no further, because there are few things in life that will give you the opportunity to change your business, career and financial future more than becoming an author.

The best of the best, the famous, and the wealthy all seem to have books. Those books have given every one of them a pay raise. Not because their books were so good, but simply *being an author* increased their credibility and opened more doors of income opportunity they may not have had otherwise.

Marketing holds a big place in creating the extent of the opportunities and wealth, but just as a foundation, having a book gives amazing benefits. Other than Internet traffic, I see nothing that increases my sales and grows my business faster than the books I have authored. You can do it, too—just make the decision and step out to get started.

"In business, you must be different to survive."

Matthew D. Miglin, PhD

~ Differentiation

Have you pulled away from the crowd and separated yourself from the masses? If not, you need to. Being liked and looking like everyone else may be more comfortable for you, but it is the beginning of a slow death for your business and income if you fit in, blend in, and are 'one of the guys.'

You need to step out of your comfort zone—look different, act differently, and speak differently than others in your industry and you'll begin to stand out. What separates you from your competition? How are your prospects remembering you? Have you identified your differentiation from your competitors? Make a list of all the differences and benefits, and build your new image and brand on why they should do business with *you*. If you don't stand out, you die. You may not die immediately, but you will die as a business sooner or later. That's why I say not to use the same old business card. Stand out with a unique approach like a book. I have yet to see anything that makes as powerful and as lasting an impression as a book. Write yours *today*.

To differentiate yourself from the competition visit:

www.ExpertSelfPublishing.com

"Do not wait for ideal circumstances; they never come".

Janet Erksine Stuart

~ Just Write Your Book

With over 83% of Americans wanting to write a book and only about 200,000 books being published each year, it appears for most it will never become a reality. Don't let that happen to you. *Just do it!* Make it happen. The rewards of being an author are great and can last a lifetime.

If you are having trouble putting your book idea together, or you just can't write, consider hiring a ghost writer. If you have most of the content in your head, you can record it as an audio file and have it transcribed. Bingo, you have an instant manuscript.

There are lots of sources that can help you make your words come to life if you look. Do your due diligence and search or *call me* and I'll will walk you through the process. Either way, the world needs to hear your message–don't disappoint them.

"Go tell the world your story; if it is good, they will seek you out for more stories."

Matthew D. Miglin, PhD

~ **Where to Start**

Start your articles or book with a blog. Yes, I said blog. A blog is not only the simplest form of a website that anyone can set up in minutes, but allows you to add daily or weekly content in just minutes with no website design knowledge.

The beauty of a blog is that you can get others to comment and interact to your submissions to create additional dialogues for your visitors. Best of all, you can use it to create the content pages of your book, one at a time, so there is no rush or pressure. Yet, because you will have followers, it will encourage you to add regular content to benefit them as well as potential prospects for your products and services.

Try setting up your blog today; you will find it easier than you would believe. Linking to your blog is also a very powerful tool to increase your website's search engine rankings. Fresh content means higher rankings, and higher search engine rankings can mean more free advertising and traffic to your website.

"A life without a purpose is like a bicycle without wheels."

Matthew D. Miglin, PhD

~ What's Your Purpose?

Before you write your book, there is one thing you need to determine before you decide on your title and content. You need to ask the question, Why? What is the *purpose* of this book? Is it to sell lots of books? To get speaking engagements? To get more clients? To make more money? To become the recognized expert in your industry? To sell more of your products or services? To boost your company's credibility?

Whatever your purpose might be, you need to determine the purpose and build your book around that purpose. Depending on your purpose, it will change how you structure your book from the cover to the content.

If the book's purpose is to help you sell a service, the content should be structured around everything related to that service, with the book promoting your service as the best compared to competitors. If your purpose is to book speaking engagements, the topic of the book should be something groups have an interest in, so groups interested in that topic will want you to speak to them about it.

Whatever your purpose, build your book on that foundation and your book will become the tool to help you reach your goals faster. Nothing great was ever accomplished without first establishing its purpose.

"Your habits are the blueprint of the life you are constructing."

Matthew D. Miglin, PhD

~ Instant Manuscript

Many of us don't have the time to spend writing our books. The average author seems to take three to seven years to get their manuscript finished. That is no longer acceptable in this information age where knowledge is doubling at alarming rates in just one or two years, consistently. We are in a FedEx day and age; we need to value time enough to compress what we need to accomplish into the same 24 hours everyone has.

Did you ever notice that the wealthy have the same amount of time as you, yet they manage to accomplish ten times what you can in the same 24 hours? Why? They compress tasks, leverage other people's money, time, and resources, and only work on the tasks in which they have the greatest gifts and strengths. If you identify your weaknesses, contract out those services to others, and focus only on doing what you are good at and enjoy doing—you will accomplish more and make much more money.

Having said that, if you are not good at writing or don't have time to write, hire a ghost writer. If you want to save time and money, speak your book into a digital recorder and have it transcribed or use software such as Dragon Naturally Speaking® that translates your words into text on your computer. There are also services like ours that will record an interview with you and transcribe it into a manuscript—72 hours later you will have most of your manuscript complete. There are no more excuses for not getting your book out if you want to be an author. Get started today with one piece of your book and just DO IT.

If you want your own instant manuscript visit:

www.ExpertSelfPublishing.com

~ How to Appear Published

In the past, self-published books *looked* self-published and very unprofessional. Only the big publishing houses had the money and equipment to make a book look and feel professionally produced. Today, unfortunately, there are still lots of self-published books that look self-published and unprofessional. But with today's unlimited resources and POD, there is no excuse for a self-published author to not have a sharp, professional-looking book.

Many new authors get lazy or go the cheap route in self-publishing their book, and, as a result, they print a book that looks self-published, is hard to sell, and lacks credibility. To the vast majority of the public, they cannot tell the difference between a traditionally-published book and a professionally-self-published book. Other than a publisher name they may or may not recognize, both books can scream credibility if done properly. There are two major mistakes most self-published authors make. The first is not hiring a professional book editor to edit the manuscript; often a book with obvious mistakes can be a dead giveaway of a self-published book. Using your wife, mother, or friend to edit is not good enough—get professionals to help.

The second area (actually the most important) is the cover design. Having a friend or even a graphic designer design your cover is not the same as using a professional *book cover designer* create and layout the front and back covers, and spine, of your book. The cover is the first impression your reader gets of your book. If it does not scream professional and credible, you've lost a sale and a future long-term client. Spend the money to do it right up front and watch your credibility and income go through the roof.

~ Entrepreneurial Publishing

Fortunately, I was an entrepreneur for two decades before I self-published my first books. That came as an advantage when I began to look at traditional vs. self-publishing vs. entrepreneurial business publishing, and it changed my life forever. I looked at who had the biggest advantages—from how I could get the biggest book advance to how I could get the biggest ROI (return on my investment).

Traditional publishing costs you $0. to produce the books. The ROI on that $0 investment is $1.00 to $1.50 per book. I guess that's okay for $0 money invested, no risk for me, but very few books are likely to be sold unless you pony up for a marketing campaign. If the average author sells fewer than 5,000 books, then you would get $5,000 to $7,500. Wow, I feel rich now. This doesn't even count the fact that you give up most of your rights as the author with traditional publishing.

When I looked at self publishing, I was shocked to find costs ranging from $295 to $35,000 with different contracts, benefits, price points, and completely different royalties or profits for the author. And, remember, marketing your book is on *your* dime. Royalties ranged from $2.00 to $8.00 per book—better than traditional publishers, but not necessarily a home run.

When I asked these self publishers if I could use a less-expensive print house to print my books if I found one, their answer was 'no.' I would need to get my own new ISBN before I could print my own books with another printer.

That is how I learned about entre-preneurial publishing—where, as the ISBN owner, I can use any printer I want to print my books, and even use multiple printers at the same time. In doing so I found I would increase my profits from a range of $1.00 to $8.00 a book to a range of $5.00 to $15.00 per book, and with an investment usually under $3,500 to get the book to print. My ROI on $3,500 and profits on 5,000 copies turns into $25,000 to $75,000—a much better return on my money, even if I only sold a few thousand books.

I can help you sell more books than that and show you how to make money *beyond* your book so your book sales will be bonus income, not your primary income. Are you ready to become an entrepreneurial publisher of your own book? It's the only way I will author my books, and you should, too.

"When authors finally grasp what TRUE self publishing means, we will see thousands of supposed self publishing companies go out of business."

Matthew D. Miglin, PhD

~ Authentic Self-Publishing

You've been lied to. Yes, the publishing industry has lied to you and spread many rumors that are not true. For example, "once you self-publish you will never be able to get a traditional publisher to consider your book" is simply untrue. I know of many authors who first self published, then were picked up by big publishing houses.

Be aware, however, that, even if you are fortunate enough to have your book picked up by a big traditional publisher, you will still be expected to shoulder most of the responsibility, and expense, of marketing your book.

I have also found the misuse of the word *self*-publishing. If you do your homework, you will find that over 95% of "self publishing companies" charge you a fee to print your book and for a variety of other services as well. The accurate term for these companies is vanity publisher.

They *say* that you retain all your rights and control, but the *truth* is that they are retaining some of the author's control and profits by holding the ISBN in their own name or issuing you an ISBN from their own bulk-purchased group of ISBNs and putting your name on it. Either way, they maintain control of all the books you print. What's worse is you are paying them to do it. And, once again, you will be shouldering the entire marketing expense for your book.

Only a small group of us are what I call **authentic self-publishers**, allowing you, the author, 100% of the control, the rights, and the profits to your book. The way you guarantee yourself control of your book is to purchase your own ISBN and then go ask your publishers if they will still print your book. This is when the truth will come out.

The difference in costs between self publishing companies varies from a fair

5–25% markup to ridiculous markups of 50– 200%. I heard a story of an author who was conned out of more than $30,000 to "self-publish" his book, and he received 3,000 hardcover copies of a book he wasn't able to sell.

Protect yourself and do your homework.

"No business will ever grow without focus, discipline, and commitment".

Matthew D. Miglin, PhD

~ Printers, Printers Everywhere

What I am about to tell you I've never heard mentioned in this industry. It is a bit radical and revolutionary in my approach to authentic self-publishing, which is where you are in 100% control of your book. When you are in control of your book and ISBN, you will want to find the best and least expensive printers for your books in quantities so you can give some of your books away to prospects, sell some for maximum profits, and provide copies to media sources and influential business people in your industry.

You want to find POD sources that can print your book for worldwide distribution, so every time an online order comes in they can instantly print the book for shipment to the purchaser. You also want to find other POD sources with different distribution connections and specialty markets. In this way, you gain instant access to new markets by using their print services. You could never do this with most self-publishing companies who demand they own the ISBN, thus limiting your market exposure.

Another good reason is that, as of spring 2008, you cannot get listed on Amazon.com anymore unless your books are produced by traditional publishers or printed through their own in-house POD source. As things change in the industry, an authentic self-published author will have the freedom to make choices and changes other authors cannot make.

Plan on using two, three, maybe even four, print sources for your book and watch your book sales explode with more opportunities and exposure than ever.

"People will naturally pay you for your information that has value."

Matthew D. Miglin, PhD

~ Generate Money for Your Book

There are lots of ways to get the money before your book comes out to pay for some of your costs, such as pre-selling your book to others or getting a commitment to buy before the book is in print.

You can sell your manuscript online as an ebook. These methods can generate sales to pay for all the production costs like cover design, editing, text layout, etc.

Why not create a recorded CD of your book and sell it online or to clients? It is easy to do and relatively inexpensive to create an income-producing product.

With a little brainstorming, you should be able to come up with ways for others to pay for your book ahead of time and, at the same time, market your services to your prospects.

These are a few ideas from a list of about 50 that I use to help authors make money to pay for publishing costs. For more details visit:

www.ExpertSelfPublishing.com

~ Save Yourself a Fortune

To save yourself a lot of money, resist the temptation of printing too many copies of your book. One of the oldest techniques printers use to increase their revenue is to get authors to give them more money by showing them how much cheaper it is per book to print in larger quantities.

Now, if you need that many or have a plan of distribution in place, maybe that would be a good move. But the end result is that you are tying your money up in a large quantity of books that might take you years to sell. You should always print a minimum number of copies, if possible. The rule of thumb is to order enough books from your printer that you are confident of selling them within 12 to 18 months. There is no excuse today to be stuck with too many books when we have the availability of print on demand as an option for getting more copies fast.

Do yourself a favor: always shop around for the best printing prices for your book. A little extra research can possibly help you find the lowest book printing prices in the market. The Internet has made this chore even easier and within a few hours you can obtain dozens of estimates from printers all over the world.

"We can do more, make more, and enjoy more when we do it together."

Matthew D. Miglin, PhD

~ Save Money with a Buddy

Do you want to write a book but don't know how? Do you find it overwhelming or maybe you don't feel qualified? If money is tight and your budget is limited, I have a solution for you. Find a buddy!

Find someone you get along with, who you like, and who has strengths you don't have—someone who would co-author a book with you. Now you have just cut your time and expenses in half. You get an automatic discount of 50% and you still get the rewards to share. I find the biggest benefits in co-authoring to be in the marketing area. You get two authors promoting and publicizing their book instead of just one. This is very powerful because although you are making 50% less profit, your ROI is still the same. Since your investment is less, your return is equally less. But in marketing, going from one to two authors is *multiple times* more effective. You get an exponential return in the end. Your ROI and profits actually are, at worst, equal to what you would make as a single author, but with much higher potential returns and profits than you would make doing it alone. There is wisdom and extreme benefit in sharing the glory with someone else.

Now this does not have to stop with two authors. You can also consider three, even four, co-authors, but you must be sure everyone has an equal heart and passion for the book. You are doing the book and yourself a disservice if someone won't carry their weight in the deal. Remember, a book can last a lifetime. Once you co-author with someone, the book forever binds you together, for good or bad.

Just as multiple authors reduce the cost to get your book in print and to market, multiple spokespersons help to sell your book to the public. Weigh taking on a co-author carefully and when you find the right person, jump in and go for it.

~ Customize Your Books

When you self-publish a book and control the rights of the book as its author, you have the opportunity to customize your book for each event, seminar, or networking group in which you'll be using the book. With the advent of print-on-demand you can make changes quickly and print 10 books or 100 books overnight and look like a genius or a hero to your group. You will appear a true professional. You can add flyers and pages to your books to fit every occasion. This really changes the dynamics of your sales conversions because it makes you look like you are the specialist dealing with their niche, even if it is your first time in front of a particular group. You will make a lasting impression that they will take home with them and be remembered over and over again.

Welcome to the new revolution of print-on-demand.

"If I could do it all over again, I would become a master at marketing and then I would pick a business."

Matthew D. Miglin, PhD

~ It's All about Marketing

Ninety percent of authors never get this important principle—that's why only 10% of authors become wealthy and profitable. Writing and publishing your book, although difficult and time consuming, is only the beginning of a successful book. It is actually the *easiest* part of being a successful author. All the work and the key to profitability of your book are in the marketing. Marketing starts *before* your book is published and continues for *years* until you want to shut off the money faucet. Marketing is not automatic; it takes a lot of work to become a profitable author, let alone a bestselling author.

New authors need to grasp this and understand that marketing is a *lifestyle* for an author—you start and don't stop until you reach your goals. Whatever budget you plan to spend on your book, expect to spend a minimum of ten times the cost of *producing* your book on *marketing* the book. Of course, more is always better. Your marketing efforts will determine how fast and far your book will get exposure and how many copies you will sell. Today it is much easier than in the past to sell lots of books, but expect to work hard to get the word out.

The next step for most authors after they learn how to self-publish their book is to discover how to self-market their book. Get hooked up with book marketing monthly memberships or programs to develop your knowledge and skills in getting your book to the masses.

Expect to commit 24 to 36 months of constant marketing and promotion, as well as ongoing marketing training, to sharpen your skills and stay up on the latest and greatest tools and techniques in the industry. Trust me on this: if you don't stay up on the latest marketing movements, it could cost you millions in missed opportunities in the marketplace.

Years ago when I was a college professor teaching eMarketing, many of the techniques I taught the students were obsolete by the end of the semester and something better and improved would have replaced it. Today, marketing is changing so fast that in order to stay relevant you need to be ready and willing to change with the flow.

It will not happen overnight, but with time and consistency you can reach your objectives and experience all the rewards of being a successful author.

Interested in staying relevant and on top of marketing changes? Visit:

www.ExpertSelfPublishing.com

"It is more blessed to give than to receive."

Acts 20:35 KJV

~ Give It Away

Most authors sell fewer than 5,000 books and make less than $25,000 in a *lifetime* on their book. The lesson to be learned here is that most of us won't get rich selling our books. But that's okay, because the real money is not *in* the book; it is the money you make *as the result of having* a book.

Since your book is the ultimate business card, why not give it away like you do a traditional business card or brochure? You don't make most of the real money off your book anyway. But the more hands your book gets into, the faster you make the real money and the more doors will open for you. If you use our printing services, for example, printing 1,000 copies of a 150-page book runs about $2.50 per copy. That's cheap enough to give away.

Now, should you also *sell* your book? Of course! You should be willing to give it away to the right prospects, in the right setting, but also sell your book to those prospects you will never see or ever meet. The power of both is an amazing combination to speed up the wealth process for you. Try it; you will be amazed at the power of giving your book away as your business card.

Let me know how it works for you. Visit www.ExpertSelfPublishing.com.

~ From Habit to Automatic

Begin today developing good habits to help you accomplish your goals automatically. If you want to have a book, it is not going to write itself. Every great accomplishment begins with a single step forward. Start something today; anything related to your goal is the place to start.

If it is writing a book, start with picking a title or brainstorming a list of possible titles. How about making an outline of potential chapters from a list of topics you want to include in your book, or just start writing the first chapter. If you *start* something, you are now one step closer to reaching your objective.

Now to make it a habit, you need to do it today, and tomorrow, and the next day, and the next, and so on for at least 21 consecutive days. *They must be consecutive*; if you miss a day, you need to start over for another 21 days.

An amazing thing will happen after 21 days: you will naturally do that habit without thinking, because it will now be automatic. It's almost miraculous how it works, but it does every time. Try it. Apply this to your goal to write and publish your book. Then it is only a matter of time before you will automatically reach your goal as a published author.

Don't wait—establish your habit today and make sure you pick the same time every day for your task. Remember consistency is the key. Just work the habit until it becomes automatic.

"The greatest men in battle or business are afraid at times but they proceed forward in spite of the fear. Now that's faith in action..."

Matthew D. Miglin, PhD

~ Do It Afraid

Are you like some people who are afraid to make a mistake or fail? Just because you may fail at something doesn't make you a failure. Napoleon Hill found in studying 178 successful men that ALL had failed *many* times before they succeeded! Isn't that amazing?

It seems falling down and getting back up are just a part of life. Not everything we try the first time will work out as well as we hoped. The key is to get back up, confront our fear, and with courage try again.

Listen, I will be honest. I made a lot of mistakes with my first book, "Home Contractor Secrets—Revealed to Homeowners." The font should have been different, the cover design should have been more attractive, I should have had more stories as examples, etc. Yet, in spite of these mistakes, the book continues to sell. Without those mistakes my other books would not be as successful. We all learn through trial and error, good and bad.

I wish it were not true, but the fastest, most effective way to succeed in anything is to fail faster and more often. You see, none of us likes to fail, so when we do we are much more motivated to make it work the next time. We will usually go the extra mile that we were not willing to push for previously.

The answer is to do it afraid and allow yourself to fail, just as long as you get back up, learn from it, and go do it again. Some of you may be terrified about writing and publishing your book. That's good, because so was every other author before you. It is just a natural part of life. Get over it and write your book *now*.

Now is the appropriate time. It is unlikely that your life will get less complex in the future, so make now the time to begin and do it. I've seen too many people write books who were not qualified and they succeeded anyway. You can succeed, too. I want to encourage you to begin the journey today toward becoming a published author and changing the world with your one-of-a-kind message.

I believe in you.

"Nothing great was ever achieved without enthusiasm."

Ralph Waldo Emerson

~ Enthusiasm, the Untapped Power

Enthusiasm is vital to success in anything in life. It is a force that cannot be fully explained, but the power that it creates is immeasurable in its capacity to change people's lives.

Next to love, there appears to be no greater source of power than that of enthusiasm directed at a single focus. Enthusiasm is most often the difference between success and failure, getting or losing a sale, prosperity or living in lack. Life is filled with impossible dreams that are only made a reality by the abundant, limitless enthusiasm carried by the dreamer expressing his heart.

A poor man with enthusiasm for a dream can become rich; a bankrupt man with enthusiasm can build an empire. Enthusiasm means, "God from within." It is like the light of God is turned on within us and we are able to obtain the impossible.

Enthusiasm is like a switch when it is turned on. People watch and listen to us and are drawn to us. It is so powerful that it can give you enough energy to miss a night's sleep and still function at your optimum level of effectiveness. Try it—get enthusiastic about your book, your business, and your dreams and watch the fruit that results. Doors will open, money will come to you, and favor with people you don't even know will become reality.

If you get enthusiastic about your purpose and your book, you will shorten your time frames and reduce many of your hurdles because of the power enthusiasm can hold in your life. Add the ingredient of enthusiasm and I guarantee your life, your business, and your finances will never be the same again.

"If you are not crystal clear, then you are blind and truly lost."

Matthew D. Miglin, PhD

~ **Focusing With Clarity**

If you are truly passionate about your book, and perhaps even desire to be a bestselling author, you *can* achieve it (or anything else for that matter) if you want it badly enough—that is, if you are willing to do whatever it takes to get it.

I am not saying you should go against your values and morals, but by staying within those parameters you can obtain what appears impossible and prove it to be possible. If you commit to becoming a bestselling author as your chief aim, you will reach it. It is through unwavering commitment and single-minded focus that you will achieve your desires.

Set it down on paper *now*—write down what the chief aim for your life is at this moment in time. Begin to make it so clear you can see every single detail of what arriving at that goal will feel like. Create such clarity to your focused goal that anyone else reading it could see what you see and create that environment in perfect detail if they were asked to do so. Clarity of focus is like a microscope so focused on one spot that it creates a clear picture of what is real but unseen by the human eye. I challenge you—if you want something, you can have it.

If you want to be a successful, well-known author, you can have it with single-minded, focused clarity. Allow your thoughts and feelings to be consumed with this desire and aim, then watch as the world opens up doors of opportunity for you that didn't exist even moments prior. The world and all that is in it is at your fingertips for you to desire and obtain, if you focus hard enough on one thing at a time. Go for it, and enjoy all it has to offer.

Would you share with me your stories and examples of how this has worked for you in your life? I'd like to know. Visit www.ExpertSelfPublishing.com.

Need more help developing your clarity? Why not order a few copies of the book I've coauthored with Dr. Wayne Dyer, Anthony Robbins and others called *"Wake Up...Live the Life You Love—Living in Clarity."* Share them with friends and colleagues.

www.LivingInClarityBook.com

~ Book Pre-Writing Checklist

Why am **I** writing this book?

What is the **purpose** of this book?

What is the **problem** I am solving?

What **pain** will I be taking away?

What is my **solution** to the problem?

What is my **target market** or niche?

What exactly does my market **want**?

How much will my target market **spend**?

What is my most important **focus**?

Can I **make enough money** in this market?

What are the **main topics** I want to cover in my book (they could be chapters)?

Do I have client **testimonies** I can use in my book?

What **title** will grab my audience's attention?

What **subtitle** will describe the benefits of the book to them?

Who can I get to **endorse** my book?

~ So You Want to Self Publish a Book

Programs we offer include:

Fast-Start Book Mentoring - *We guide you one on one*

Hands-Off Authoring - We can do it <u>all</u> for you

Manuscript-to-Print – We take you from rough manuscript to the printer

Editing – We provide all levels of editing services

Layout and Design – We design your book covers and interior layout

Proofing – We provide full proofreading services

Instant Manuscript – We interview you and transcribe your manuscript for you

Book Printing – We work with printers to get you the best deal

Book Marketing Mentorship-We guide you one on one

Exclusive Membership - *Community membership*

For pricing and details::

visit www.ExpertSelfPublishing.com,

call toll free at 866-316-3700, or

email Support@ExpertSelfPublishing.com.

~ A Gift for You

The Ultimate Business Card will help grow your business and your income better, faster and easier by revealing how to effectively self-publish you and your books.

We want to share a free gift with you by visiting us at:

www.TheUltimateBusinessCard.net

or call toll free 866-316-3700.

~ Matt Miglin's FREE Business Resources List

Shopping cart

Domain Names

Website Hosting

Membership sites

Set up your company

Audio tools

Virtual Assistants

Press releases

Marketing tools

Blogging

Podcasting

Keyword searching

Money management

www.MattMiglin.com/resources

~ Matthew D. Miglin, PhD

Matthew is a forward-thinking entrepreneur, author, self-publishing business expert, and inspiring speaker. He offers exceptional business wisdom, gained through 27 years of business development, training, and management experience, directing operations for several successful entrepreneurial endeavors.

Matthew is the President of Voice of Prosperity, LLC —a self-publishing, training, consulting, and educational resources company that specializes in helping individuals and businesses to grow, prosper, self publish, and lead more fulfilling lives.

He has presented well-received and profit-enhancing business seminars to individuals, businesses, schools, and government agencies. And he is a Certified Seminar Leader through American Seminar Leaders Association.

Matthew has excelled in the past as President of a multi-million-dollar building and remodeling firm, with a proven track record of increasing profits, production, and doubling sales over three consecutive years.

He developed extensive leadership skills under challenging circumstances while serving in the United States Marine Corps and during Operation Desert Storm.

In addition, he is the author and co-author of multiple books, ebooks, CDs, DVDs, and info-products such as:

Wake Up...Live the Life You Love: Living In Clarity

The Six-Figure Contractor

Practical Kingdom Prosperity

Self Publishing Secrets

People to People Marketing

Home Contractor Secrets—Revealed to Home Owners

Business God's Way

How to Hire the Right Contractor

Matthew holds his doctorate in Business Development from Cambridge International University and his bachelor's and master's degrees in Business Administration from American State University.

~ Notes and Breakthroughs

_____

_____

_____

_____

_____

_____

_____

_____

_____

_____

_____

~ Notes and Breakthroughs